PASSOVER ON EVEREST

by **Rachelle Burk** · *illustrated by* **Craig Orback**

On a family trip to Israel, Nikki Bart treks up the curvy path of Mount Masada, trying to keep up with her mother, Cheryl. The peak looks so far away! The sun beats down. Her legs ache.

When she finally reaches the top, the view makes
her belly flutter. She slips her hand into Mum's.

She did it!

Nikki and her mother climb more mountains together, at home in Australia and on vacations abroad. The challenge excites Nikki. Each time she stands on a summit, she feels she can do anything.

Her family talks about the importance of mountains to the Jewish people: God spoke to Abraham on Mount Moriah.

Moses received the Ten Commandments on Mount Sinai.

Jews rebelled against the Roman Army on Mount Masada. Climbing mountains feels sacred to Nikki.

At Passover, Nikki's favorite holiday, her family recounts the ancient Israelites' flight to freedom.

As the meal is served, her aunts, uncles, cousins, and grandparents want to hear about her adventures. They talk, laugh, and sing until late in the evening. Nikki loves her family's holiday gatherings, even more than climbing mountains.

When Nikki is 16, she and Mum set an ambitious goal: to climb the highest mountain on each of the seven continents.

Within a few years, they conquer the first six peaks. Few birds ever reach such heights.

MOUNT DENALI
MOUNT ELBRUS
MOUNT EVEREST
MOUNT KILIMANJARO
MOUNT KOSCIUSZKO

In the spring of 2008, Nikki and her mother arrive in Asia for their final challenge. They will scale the world's highest peak—Mount Everest!

The quest is ambitious . . . and dangerous.

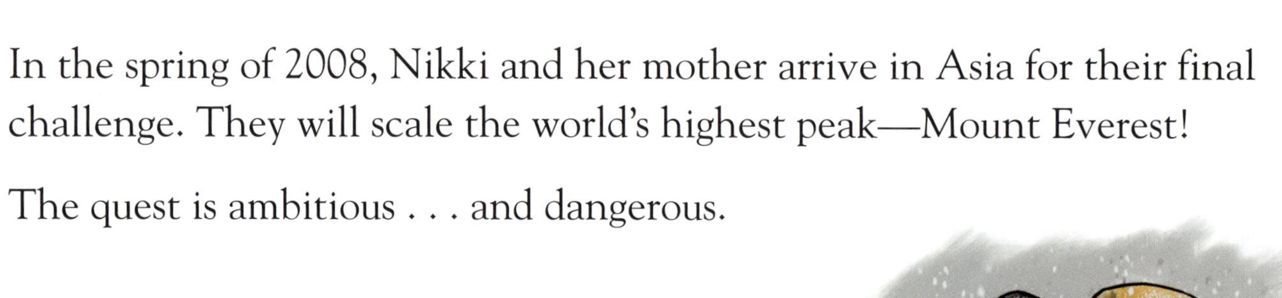

The air, so high up, is low in oxygen, which makes it hard to breathe.

Frigid temperatures cause many climbers to lose fingers, toes, or the tip of their nose to frostbite. One misstep can send a mountaineer tumbling. But Nikki has confidence. Courage. Faith.

Only one thing dampens Nikki's spirits. Although spring is the safest time of year to climb Mount Everest, it is also the Passover season. This year, instead of spending the Passover seder with family, she and Mum will be on an icy slope surrounded by strangers. Nikki brushes away the thought.

The two women recite the *Tefilat Haderech*—the traveler's prayer asking God to watch over them and their team as they begin their trek.

With their sherpa guides—highly trained Nepali mountaineers—the climbing team arrives eleven days later at the base of Mount Everest.

Already they are higher than two thousand flights of stairs! Yet they still have far to go before they reach the top of the mighty mountain.

Every day they make difficult treks back and forth from Base Camp.

This prepares
them for the
challenging climb
to the peak, and
helps their bodies
adapt to high
altitude.

The Jewish holiday approaches. "Thinking about Passover
makes me a little homesick," says Nikki.
"Me, too," Mum admits.
The lead sherpa overhears her. "What is Passover?" he asks.

Nikki and her mother tell him about the holiday. They describe the foods on the seder plate—the mix of apples, nuts, and wine called *charoset*, a hard-boiled egg, lamb bone, bitter horseradish, and parsley. Nikki explains what each food symbolizes in the Passover story of hardship, hope, and new beginnings.

The sherpa asks more questions about the holiday. To Nikki, this makes him seem less like a stranger and more like a friend.

A week later, on the first night of Passover, Nikki is tired. Her muscles ache from days of hard trekking to and from Base Camp. Thoughts drift to her family, gathering for the seder without them…

Dad setting the table, with a *Haggadah*—the Passover book—placed at every seat.

Mother and daughter must settle for nibbling the bit of matzah they brought along. Nikki feels sad and very far from home.

One of the guides approaches Nikki and Cheryl as they prepare their gear for tomorrow's trek. "Dress in your best for dinner tonight," he says with a wink.

Their best? What's going on? The two pull on fresh sweaters and their cleanest thermal underwear.

When they enter the meal tent, everyone smiles. At first, Nikki doesn't understand why. Then she notices the table. Her eyes grow wide.

The sherpas have prepared
a Passover feast! Chicken soup and lamb.
Hard-boiled eggs. Chopped apples and walnuts.
They have baked a type of matzah—a local
unleavened bread called *chapati*. There are even
candles and wine, all carried up the mountain
for the special Jewish holiday celebration.
Nikki's eyes well up with joy.

Mum's face glows as she lights the candles and recites a Passover blessing.
Their climbing companions from around the world urge Nikki and
Cheryl to tell them about the holiday.

The women tell the story of their ancestors' journey from oppression to freedom, and of another mountaineer—Moses—receiving God's commandments on Mount Sinai.

Nikki imagines her family and friends at home around the seder table, telling the same story and reciting the same blessings. Although they are oceans away, she feels close to them.

Nikki recites the traditional "Four Questions."

Ma nishtana, ha-layla ha-zeh, mi-kol ha-lelot. . .
How is this night different from all other nights?

Surrounded by a different sort of family, feeling a different sort
of freedom, she could think of so many ways.

For all the Dreamers, Adventurers and Explorers

We reflect on our important relationships with the mountains, the natural world and each other. We believe that climbing is not about "conquering" a mountain but rather about our relationship with her. You can't control the weather, the conditions or your health, but you can control the choice to be there, remain in the present and how you will deal with difficult and/or unexpected conditions.

We also learned so much about ourselves—how to manage in adversity, commitment, teamwork, resilience and taking personal responsibility. We met so many special people and learned about greatly different and unique cultures and customs. And even shared a very important Jewish festival and customs with our friends on Everest.

Our relationship with the mountains has given us so much knowledge, wisdom and joy. We have experienced awe and wonder. We hope you do too.

The summit of a mountain feels like being in the "holy of holies," a place so spiritual you feel deeply connected. We are grateful to have gone on this spiritual and physical journey together and are glad it has been documented in this children's book so we can share it with our daughter/granddaughter. L'dor Vador—From generation to generation....

—Cheryl and Nikki

Date	Continent	Mountain	Country	Altitude above sea level
July 2000:	AUSTRALIA	Mount Kosciuszko	(Australia)	7,310 ft (2,228m)
June 2003:	AFRICA	Mount Kilimanjaro	(Tanzania)	19,340 ft (5,895m)
June 2004:	EUROPE	Mount Elbrus	(Russia)	15,230 ft (5,642m)
Dec. 2004:	ANTARCTICA	Mount Vincent		16,050 ft (4,892m)
Jan. 2005:	SOUTH AMERICA	Aconcagua	(Argentina)	22,838 ft (6,961m)
May 2006:	NORTH AMERICA	Mount Denali	(USA)	20,310 ft (6,190m)
May 2008:	ASIA	Mount Everest	(Nepal)	29,032 ft (8,849m)

AUTHOR'S NOTE

Nicole "Nikki" Bart was five years old when she ascended Israel's Masada, the first mountain she climbed with her mother, Cheryl. That experience sparked her passion for mountaineering.

The two women are the first mountaineers to have had a Passover seder on Mount Everest. The sherpas, who practice Buddhism, understood Nikki and Cheryl's need to feel connected to their religion during an important holiday, and went to great lengths to make it happen. The display of cross-cultural solidarity from all the members of their climbing team touched the women deeply.

Nikki and Cheryl are the only mother-daughter team to have successfully scaled Mount Everest. When they completed their Seven Summits challenge, fewer than 250 people world wide had achieved that feat.

After Mount Everest, their adventures continued. In 2011, the pair skied to the North Pole. In 2018, they climbed Mount Sidley, the tallest volcano in Antarctica. Only 40 people in the world had successfully climbed it before them.

Nikki is now a heart doctor in Sydney, Australia. Cheryl is a lawyer and company director.

THE PASSOVER HOLIDAY

PASSOVER is a week-long holiday, celebrated in the spring, when the Jewish people read the story of the Jewish slaves escaping from Egypt. The festival begins with a *seder*, a festive meal that includes prayers, readings and songs, and the tasting of symbolic foods.

Matzah: An unleavened bread that reminds us that when enslaved Jews fled Egypt, they had no time for their bread to rise. They took the raw dough on their journey and baked it into hard crackers called matzah.

Charoset: A mixture of apples and nuts that represents the clay the slaves used to make bricks. It is a reminder of how hard the slaves worked.

Maror (horseradish): "Bitter herbs," which remind us of the bitterness of slavery.

Hard-Boiled Egg: A symbol of spring, hope and the circle of life.

Lamb: A lamb bone on the seder plate symbolizes the sacrifices the Jews had to make to gain freedom.

Parsley: Dipped in salt water, this green herb is a reminder that spring has come, a season of renewed life. The *salt water* recalls the tears of the slaves.

Passover Wine: A symbol of freedom. The ritual spilling of drops of wine during the seder is a reminder of ten plagues that God sent to punish Pharaoh.

Passover Candles: A reminder of the importance of keeping the flame of freedom alive in the world.

The Four Questions: The traditional questions asked about specific Passover rituals, which serve as a starting point for telling the Passover story.

About the Author

Rachelle Burk writes fiction and nonfiction books for children ages 1-13. Among her other Jewish-themed picture books are *Space Torah: Astronaut Jeffrey Hoffman's Cosmic Mitzvah, She's a Mensch! Jewish Women Who Rocked the World, A Mitzvah for George Washington, Matzah Ball Chase,* and *The Best Four Questions.* She has also published many secular titles, including *A Gift of Life: A Story of Organ and Tissue Donation, The Story of Taylor Swift,* and *Stomp, Wiggle, Clap, and Tap: My First Book of Dance.* A retired social worker, Rachelle is also a children's entertainer, performing as Tickles the Clown and Mother Goof Storyteller. She loves to share her love of reading and writing by visiting elementary schools around the country. You can find out more about her books and school visits at rachelleburk.com.

About the Artist

Craig Orback is the illustrator of over 20 published books for children, including *Space Torah: Astronaut Jeffrey Hoffman's Cosmic Mitzvah, Starring Steven Spielberg: The Making of a Young Filmmaker, Born to Draw Comics: The Story of Charles Schulz and the Creation of Peanuts,* and the Charlotte Award and Keystone to Reading Book Award winning title *The Can Man.* Craig lives near Seattle, WA, and loves to share his books with students during school and library visits. At the age of 15 he climbed Mt. Whitney, the highest peak in the continental U.S., with his dad. He invites you to visit him online at craigorback.com.

Text copyright © 2025 Rachelle Burk
Jacket art and interior illustrations © 2025 Intergalactic Afikoman
Designed by Elynn Cohen

Intergalactic Afikoman
1037 NE 65th Street, #164
Seattle, WA 98115

www.IntergalacticAfikoman.com

Names: Burk, Rachelle, author. | Orback, Craig, illustrator.

Title: Passover on Everest / by Rachelle Burk; illustrated by Craig Orback.

Description: First edition. | Seattle: Intergalactic Afikoman, [2025] | Interest age level: 004-008. | Summary: In
                  this true story about kindness across cultures, Jewish mother-daughter mountain climbing team Cheryl
                  and Nikki Bart experience a seder like no other—a seder on Mt. Everest, the highest mountain in the
                  world!—Publisher.

Identifiers: ISBN: 978-1-951365-28-8

Subjects: LCSH: Bart, Cheryl—Juvenile literature. | Bart, Nikki—Juvenile literature. | Women mountaineers—
                  Australia—Biography—Juvenile literature. | Jewish women—Biography—Juvenile literature.
                  Passover—Juvenile literature. | Kindness—Juvenile literature. | Everest, Mount (China and Nepal)—
                  Description and travel—Juvenile literature. | CYAC: Bart, Cheryl. | Bart, Nikki. | Mountaineers—
                  Biography—Australia. | Jewish women—Biography. | Passover. | Kindness. | Everest, Mount (China
                  and Nepal)—Description and travel. | LCGFT: Biographies. | BISAC: JUVENILE NONFICTION /
                  Biography & Autobiography / Women. | JUVENILE NONFICTION / Holidays & Celebrations /
                  Passover. | JUVENILE NONFICTION / Religion / Judaism.

Classification: LCC: GV199.9 .B87 2025 | DDC: 796.5220922—dc23

                  Library of Congress Control Number: 2024946704

                  Printed in the USA
                  First Edition

                  2 4 6 8 10 9 7 5 3 1